Praying Our Father in Cree and English

By Sylvia Caribou

Copyright © 2017 Sylvia Caribou

All rights reserved. No portion of this book may be reproduced in any form without permission from the publisher, except as permitted by Canadian and U.S.A. copyright law. For permissions contact Sylvia Caribou

The advice and strategies found within may not be suitable for every situation. This work is sold with the understanding that neither the author nor the publisher are held responsible for the results accrued from the advice in this book.

ISBN-13: 978-0-9958408-2-9

DEDICATION

Especially to my dear parents Mr. Adam Castel and Mrs. Domithilde Castel. Friends and family. My hope is that you use this prayer for you and your family. Teaching your child how to pray is very important. I was taught to pray in Cree and English growing up with my parents. We would pray every morning and evening that's just the way my parents were. They loved to pray.

Now I am sending this message to everyone that is reading this book. Please allow your children to pray in Cree or English and learn about God, he is great and we all need God in our lives one time or another. May God bless you all!!

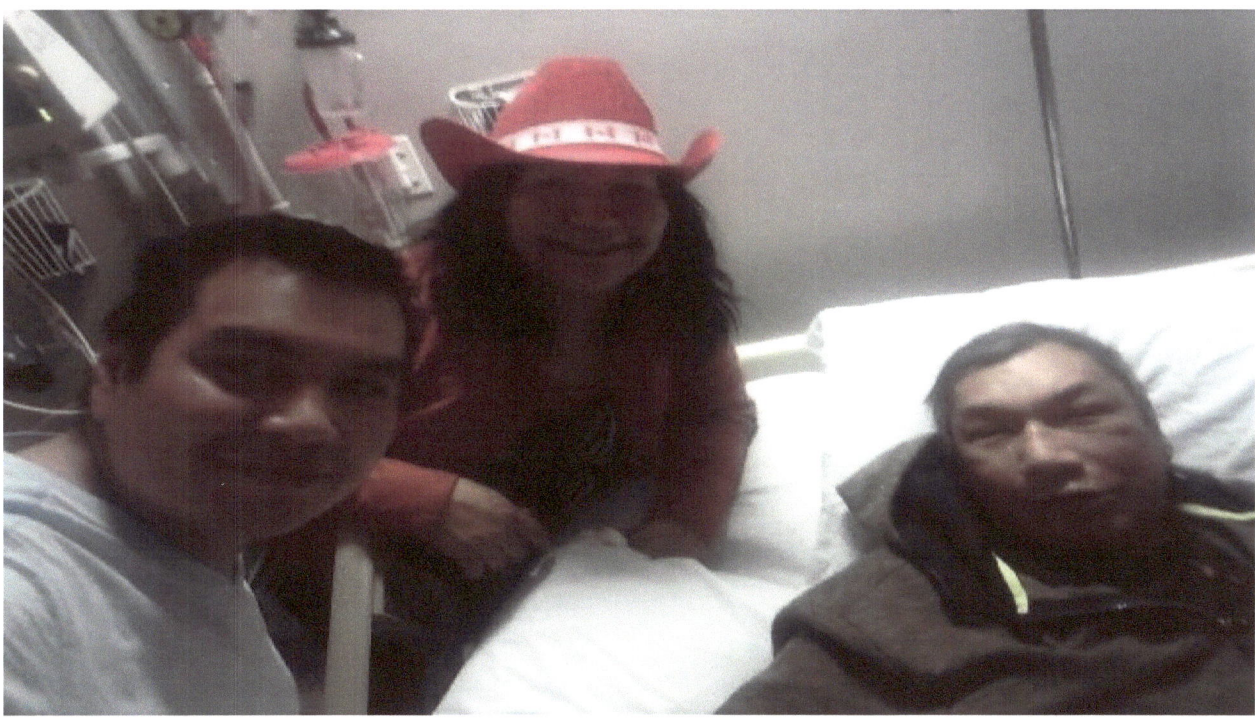

Left to right: Robert Robinson, Sylvia Caribou, and Steve Castel

ACKNOWLEDGEMENTS

Elder Christina Linklater has inspired me to learn about our traditional ways of life.

Thanks also to Cornelius Bighetty for this translation work and to the staff of the Pukatawagan Regional Centre, University College of the North, Ralph Caribou, coordinator, and to Janice Seto, instructor of the diploma in Community Economic Development program.

Our Father

Notawinan

Families gathering to see their little ones getting baptised

Which art in heaven

Kayayan kischikisikohk ite

John Dumas at the far end, looking at Wilma Linklater to the far right. Elder Ann Colomb with her jacket half way down, sitting with Elder Matilda Linklater.

Hallowed be thy name

naspit kiwithowin

That's me there looking and Elder Mary Ann Dumas and Tyrone Caribou(jr) looking to the left.

Thy Kingdom come

Kitipethchikewin, kitithetamowin Misiwe ochichipathe,

Sylvia Caribou and Niomi Sinclair with baby.
Tyrone Caribou(sr) behind the baby.

Thy will be done on earth

Tawitochikatew ota ashihk

Sylvia Caribou doing the first reading.

As it is in heaven

Tapiskotch katochikatek kihchikisikohk

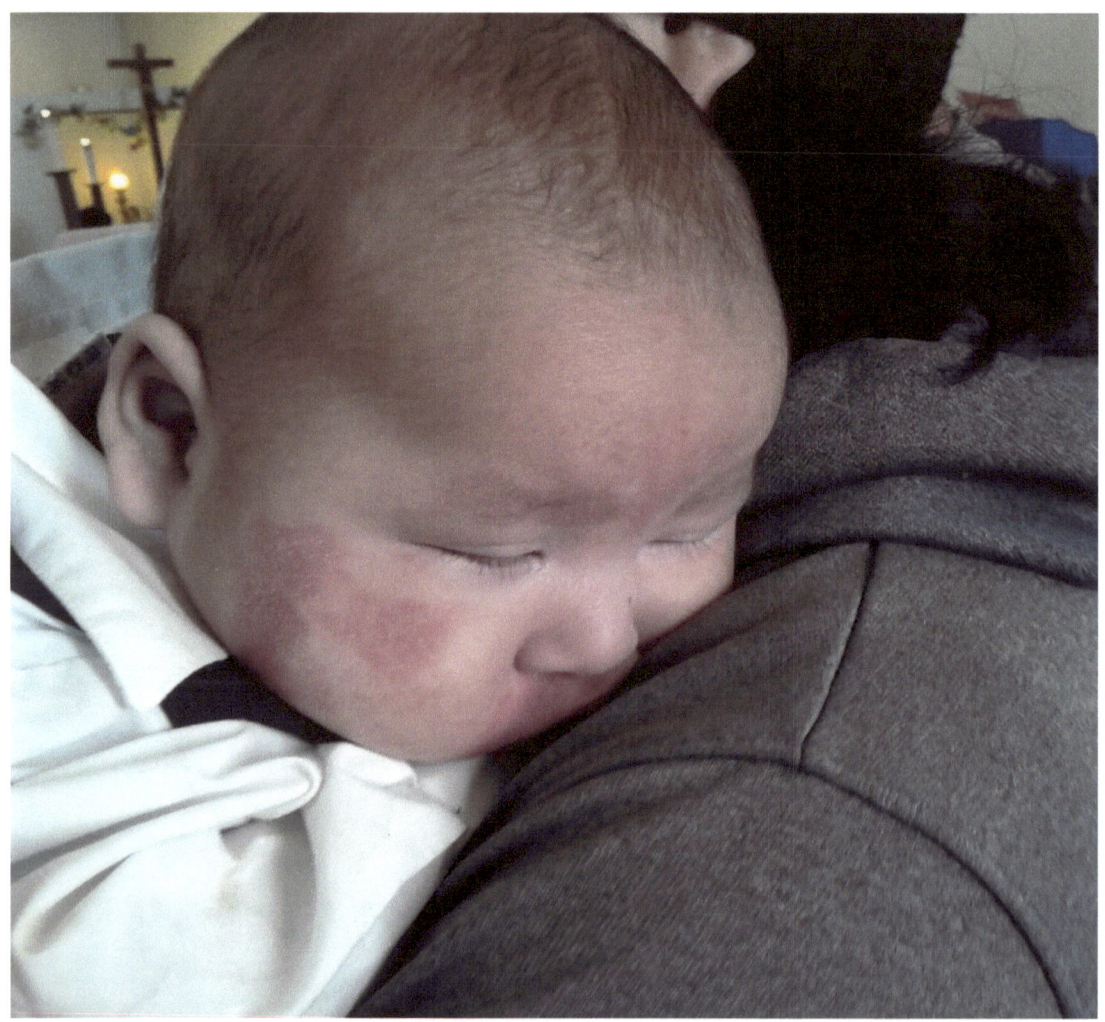

Baby John Adam Eli Colomb and Mom Ashley Dumas

Give us this day

Mithinan anotch kakisikak

Baptism towards the ending

Our daily bread

Nikisikani pahkwesikanimiana

Father Dani having baptism for all these wonderful, beautiful babies of Pukatawagan Mb.

And forgive us our trespasses

Ekwa pinatamawinan ita kepiwanitotamak

Father D with Elder Hilda Francois

As we forgive those Who trespass against us

Tapiskotch ka-isi pimathitotahaweyaokohk

Eli Castel Looking at something and Baby Precious watching her grandpa Eli

And lead us not into temptation

Oki kakipe wanitotakaweya

Baby Precious Castel and Grandpa Eli Castel to the left

But deliver us from evil

Kawitha itapekinan ita ka-itakohk mistahi machikakwachihiwawin

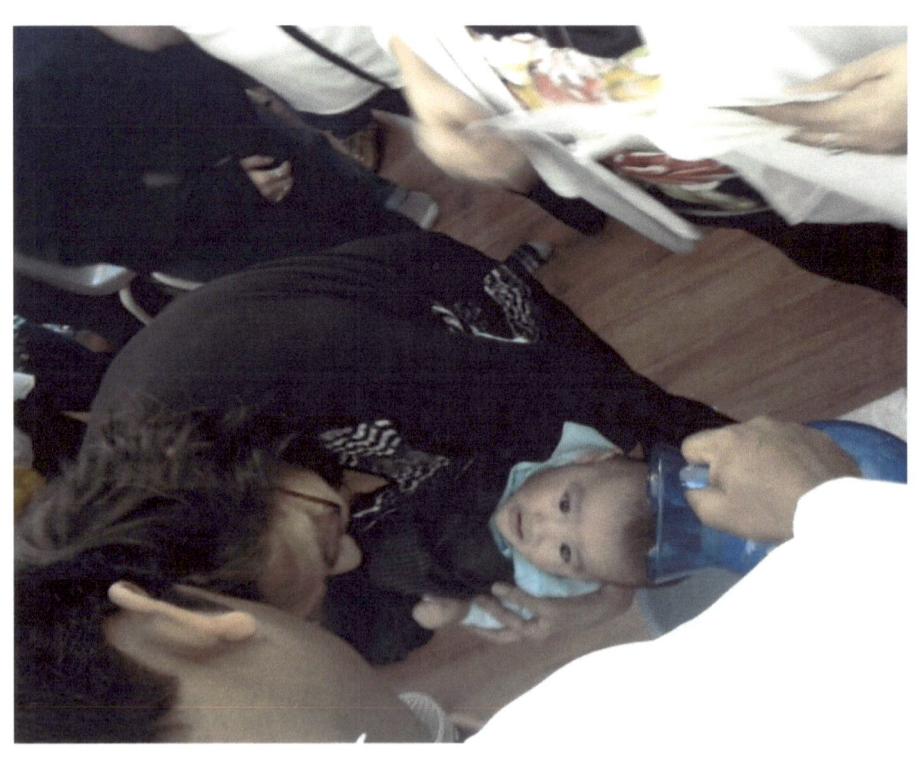

God Mother-Elizabeth Bear holding Baby Bryson Castel

For thine is the kingdom

Maka wikatenina anta-och machipimatisiwinihk

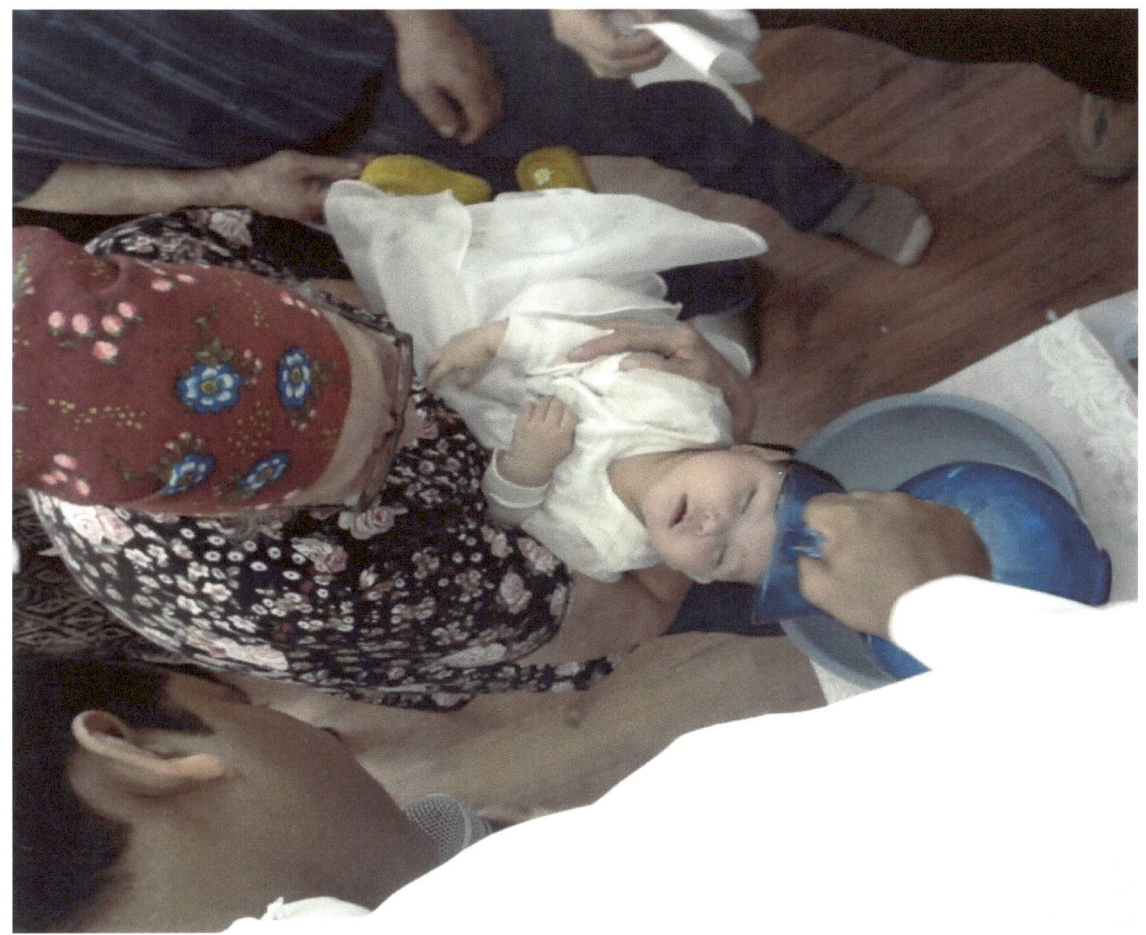

Elder Flora Grieves with her God Child

The power and the glory

Kitipitheten kakithow kekwan sokatisiwin asichi Mithewthitamowin

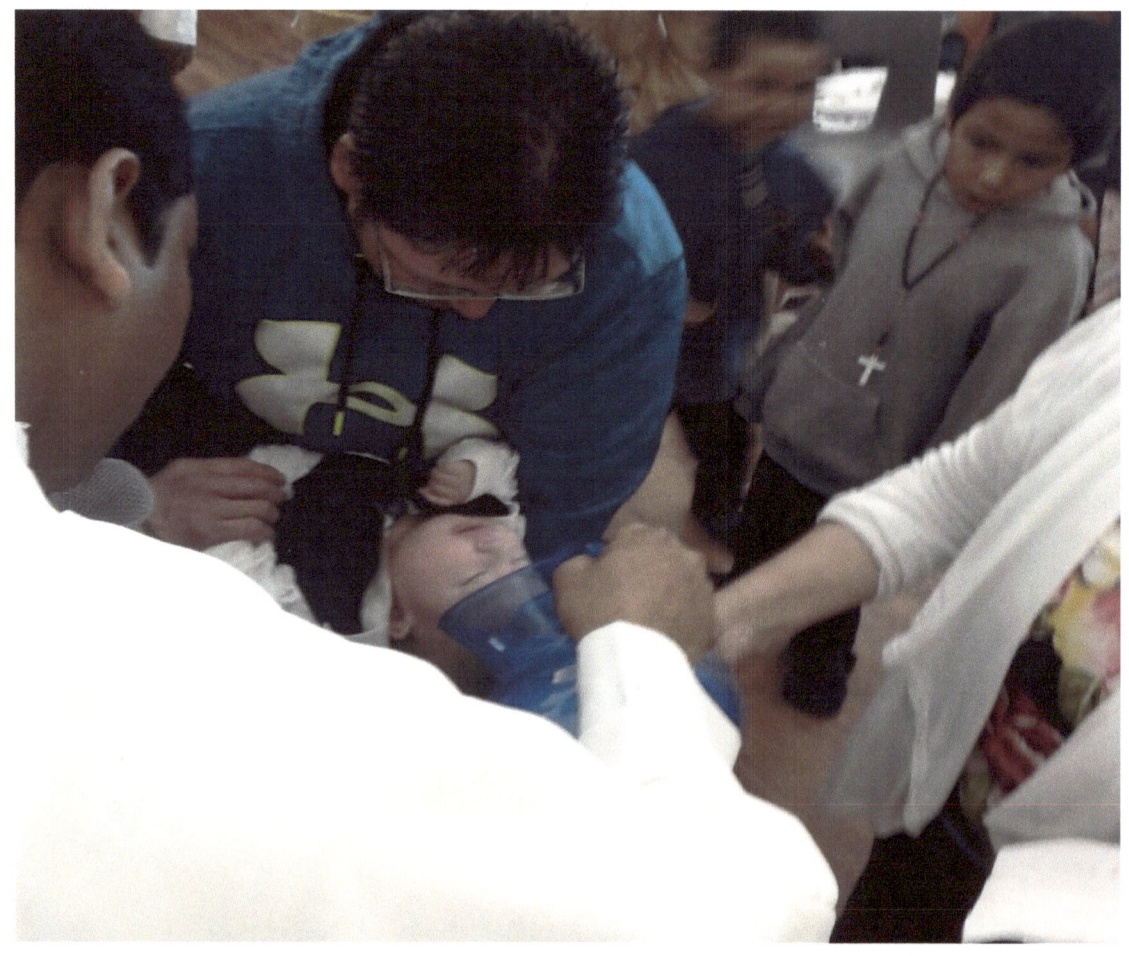

Josephine Dumas with her God child Little AJ-

Now and forever and ever

Anotch mina kakike

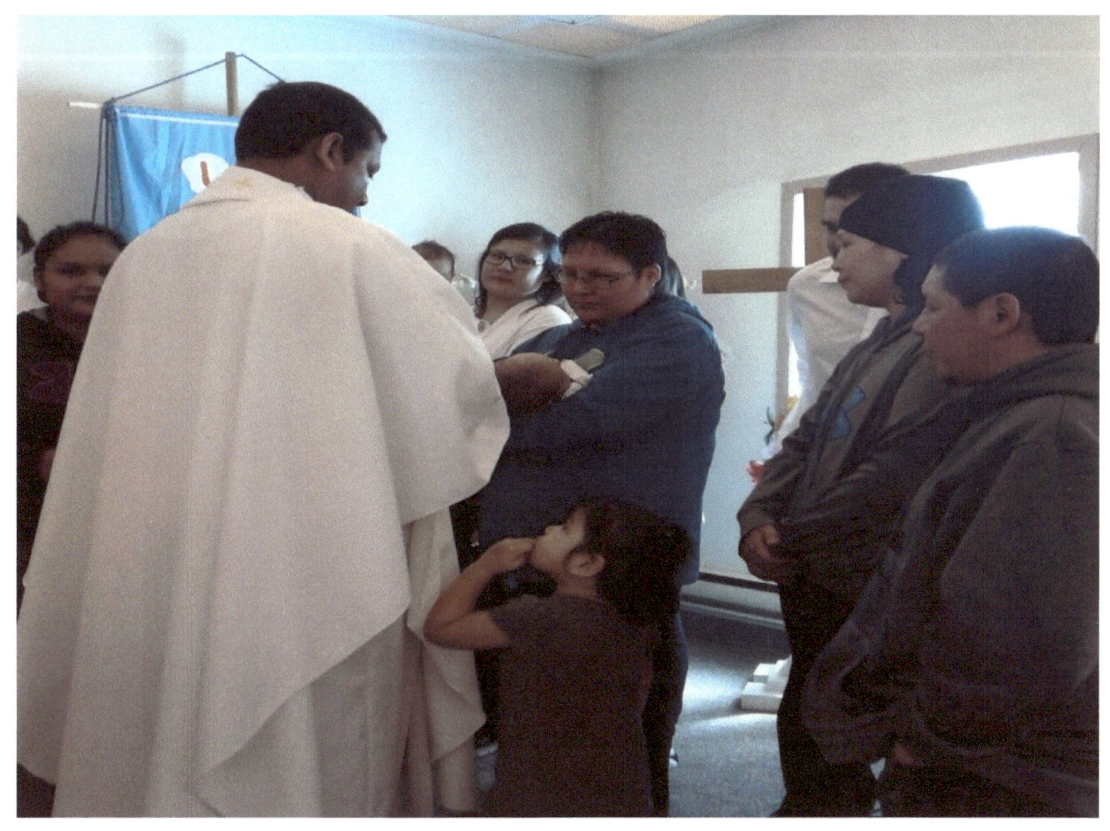

Josephine Dumas holding her god child AJ with Mom Ashley Dumas and God father Tom Caribou to the right

Amen

Tanikoshi

Tazi's first baptism

In the name of the father

Ohtawininhet

Bruno Bighetty holding the cross with Flora and Oliver Grieves to the left. And the little girl holding the candle is

And of the son

Ohkisokowinhet

Corieen Castel holding baby precious with husband Steven Castel and their boys, Maris and Cade. And Sylvia Caribou

And of the holy spirit

Meyosimantou

Holding the candle Miss Darylin Linklater, Father Dhana Amarlapudi, Wally Caribou, and Marilyn Hart/Castel far right.

Amen

Tanikosi

Trina Castel and Elizabeth Bear looking at something.

Be happy

Methewthitamok

Mass has ended, everyone holding their candles up for the babies.

Pray anywhere

Pikewte ayamiha

Mass has ended. Everyone getting ready for the baptism feast.

Number of prayers once in the morning and once at night

Mamiskota mechet ayamehowwina peyakow ekekisipiyak ekwa peyakow ate atakosik

Teaching prayer to help kids grow

Takiskinahamowachik ayamihowin awasisak ta wichehachik awasisak ati opikechick

Jamie Caribou with big sister Ciara Caribou

Church of Pukatawagan
Ayamihekamik pakitahoguni

New church was built in the late 1990's

Famous sign of Pukatawagan

Pakitahoguni

Home of the famous Sidney Castel(sr) 'The Pukatawagan Song' featured on The Tonight Show with Jimmy Fallon

https://www.youtube.com/watch?v=xEetps8YwF4

ABOUT THE AUTHOR

Praying Our Father in Cree and English

A member of Mathias Colomb Cree Nation in northern Manitoba, Canada, Sylvia Caribou is the third youngest of 13 children, born and raised in Pukatawagan, Manitoba. She graduated from Kelsey Learning High School in The Pas, Manitoba and holds a diploma in Social Development Management from Yellow Quill College Winnipeg, Manitoba. She is active with her family, community, and a new writing career.

With a background in canoe racing, Sylvia's first book (also available on Amazon) is about the Missinippi Challenge, the annual canoe race from Sandy Bay, Saskatchewan to Pukatawagan, Manitoba. Sylvia and her brother Napoleon Castel, entered the inaugural race as a mixed team in 1988. It was a grueling 13 hours from start to finish. And they won 3rd place in the mixed category.

For her, it's all about completing the race and endurance.

www.ingramcontent.com/pod-product-compliance
Lightning Source LLC
Chambersburg PA
CBHW041229040426
42444CB00002B/109